Clive keeps his Cool

MICHAELA MORGAN

Illustrated by Dee Shulman

OXFORD
UNIVERSITY PRESS

OXFORD
UNIVERSITY PRESS

Great Clarendon Street, Oxford OX2 6DP

Oxford University Press is a department of the University of Oxford.
It furthers the University's objective of excellence in research, scholarship,
and education by publishing worldwide in

Oxford   New York

Auckland   Cape Town   Dar es Salaam   Hong Kong   Karachi
Kuala Lumpur   Madrid   Melbourne   Mexico City   Nairobi
New Delhi   Shanghai   Taipei   Toronto

With offices in

Argentina   Austria   Brazil   Chile   Czech Republic   France   Greece
Guatemala   Hungary   Italy   Japan   Poland   Portugal   Singapore
South Korea   Switzerland   Thailand   Turkey   Ukraine   Vietnam

Oxford is a registered trade mark of Oxford University Press
in the UK and in certain other countries

British Library Cataloguing in Publication Data
Data available

ISBN: 978-0-19-917994-7

15 17 19 20 18 16

Available in packs
Stage 12 Pack of 6:
ISBN: 978-0-19-917993-0
Stage 12 Class Pack:
ISBN: 978-0-19-919968-6
Guided Reading Cards also available:
ISBN: 978-0-19-919970-9

Cover artwork by Dee Shulman
Photograph of Michaela Morgan © Richard Drewe

Printed in Malaysia by
MunSang Printers Sdn Bhd

Paper used in the production of this book is a natural, recyclable product
made from wood grown in sustainable forests. The manufacturing process
conforms to the environmental regulations of the country of origin.

Chapter 1

Here's Clive.

Clive ran all the way to school.
It was a sunny day.
In fact it was:

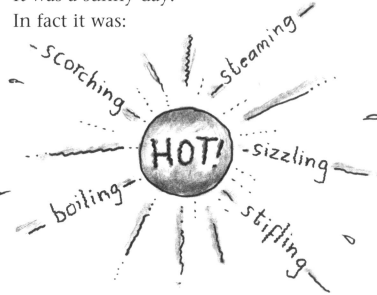

Clive could feel the pavement heat
beneath his feet. He could feel the air
hot and heavy on his head.

Down the street he went.

puff puff puff

Over the bridge he went.

pant pant pant

Round the corner he went and

← there was the school.

And there was the bus.
All ready to take Clive's
class to the farm park.

And there was his teacher, Miss Strictly. She was holding the register and marking it as everyone got on.

Clive could see Barry and Gary, and Sally and Sue, Dilip and David, Debjani too and Joanne and some others, plus a few helpful mothers and one or two teachers too.

Yes, they were all there and
they were all getting on
the bus.

'Hey, wait for me,'
      yelled Clive.

Where's Clive?

But then the bus doors closed.
The bus engine revved up.
No one heard him… and
the bus pulled away.

Chapter 2

Clive stood on the corner. He felt like crying. What should he do?

Should he go into school?

Should he go back home?

Should he stay where he was?

What could he do?

It looked like Clive was…

…out of breath,	out of luck and…	…up to his neck in

Or was he?

He watched the bus pulling away.
He heard the children give a goodbye cheer and then…

…the bus made a funny little HICCUP and a splutter and… SSSTOPPED

The doors opened and the driver and Miss Strictly got out. Miss Strictly was getting cross.

'Don't you worry,' said the driver. 'This old bus won't let us down. It's just not used to the heat, that's all. I'll give it a drop of water and we'll be off.'

No problems

Clive took his chance.
He sprinted forward
and slid onto the bus.

Made it!

Cool as a cat, he plumped himself
down on the front seat.

Hey Clive!

You made it!

Miss Strictly was still sighing and
tut-tutting as she got back
on the bus.
She settled
back into
her seat.

Unfortunately it was the same seat
Clive had just plumped himself down on.

AAAGHHHH!

It was difficult to tell who screamed the loudest.

It could have been Clive.

It could have been the other children.

But it was probably Miss Strictly. She shot straight up in the air, hit her head on the roof, and then turned to see what she'd sat on.

Sorry, Miss—

Accident, Miss.

Clive blushed.

He moved to the back of the bus and squeezed in next to his friends.

Come on Clive!

The engine revved again. The bus moved away and everyone cheered.

HOORAY!

We're off!

—Again!

Chapter 3

Dilip and David explored their packed lunches. Clive explored *his* packed lunch. It had been a bit squashed by Miss Strictly sitting on it.

He tried to punch it back into shape.

The crisps and the chicken were a bit **flat**

and the biscuits were in tiny little crumbs

Luckily, not even Miss Strictly could completely flatten a can of cola.

Clive was hot after all that running.

He needed a drink.

He pulled the ring to open the can.

Now you know what happens to fizzy drinks if you shake them up and down, don't you?

You know what happens to fizzy drinks when you run about with them, don't you?

You know what happens if you open a can of shaken up and down fizzy drink on a bus?

It happened.

Sshhh!

went the can quietly as if it was trying to tell him something, but Clive carried on and...

Miss Strictly turned and saw Clive sitting in a puddle of cola, with an empty drink can in his hand.

Clive went up to the front.
Everyone stared at him.
Sally giggled.

Gary laughed
as Clive
squelched
by him.

Clive felt hotter than ever.
He was stickier than ever.
He was thirstier than ever.
And now he had no drink
left.

Chapter 4

It was stuffy on the bus.

The back of Clive's legs stuck to the seat, but even so Clive sat still and quiet and good next to Miss Strictly. Behind him Sally started singing.

Everyone joined in, except Gary. He was busy eating. He'd got through:

before Miss Strictly spotted him.

Gary never touched his sandwiches.
He always swopped them for someone
else's crisps.

Sally and her group were singing.

But after they'd got to twenty-two
men and their dog went to mow a
meadow, they stopped.

Joanne said,

'This is the *real* countryside,' said Miss Strictly.

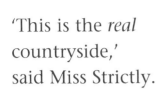

Look at the views!

But, after a while, nearly everyone agreed with Joanne.

Views are boring.

Are we nearly there, Miss?

I need the toilet, Miss.

I feel a bit sick Miss.

And I really need a drink!

But the bus rolled on and on and on…

Chapter 5

At last they arrived at

Miss Strictly glared at everyone.

Everyone got out and s t r e t c h e d in their own way.

David dashed off to the toilets.

Sally skipped off to see the lambs.

Aaaah, cute!

GENTS

But Clive had spotted something far more interesting.

An ICE CREAM van.

He raced off and queued up in a very,

very,

very,

long

queue.

At last Clive got to the front but Gary pushed in.

Clive didn't want Gary to push in. And Clive didn't want to swop his crisps. A bit of a scuffle broke out and...

...the ice cream man got cross.

And so Clive was a bit late

... and a bit messy

and Miss Strictly
was not happy
with him.

Miss Strictly took
a deep breath.

Now we can get started.
Gather round and listen.
Mr Twaddle is going to
tell you all about cows,
sheep and goats.

COWS, SHEEP & GOATS
— THE FACTS —

Chapter 6

Everyone gathered round and looked at Mr Twaddle. A few sheep and goats gathered round and looked at the children.

Ahem–

'Is everyone listening?' said Mr Twaddle. Everyone nodded, except Clive.

Clive licked his lolly.
It was cool. It was tingly.
It was orange. It was zingy.
It was... annoying Miss Strictly.

'Listen carefully,' she said.

No wriggling, no fidgeting and NO EATING!

She glared at Clive as she said this.

So Clive stood as still and quiet as he could. He listened very carefully and held his lolly tightly behind his back.

But although he tried his best he couldn't stand very still when someone was Pushing and shoving behind him.

Clive did his best, but he couldn't keep absolutely quiet when he felt a funny wet tickling on his hand.

Clive did his very best, but he couldn't help fidgeting and wriggling just a little bit as he felt more and more tickling on his hands.

And he couldn't help giggling when he saw Gary and Sally giggling and sniggering too.

Clive waited as long as he could but he couldn't help trying for a quick lick of his lolly when no one was looking.

Unfortunately he couldn't help yelling out

when he saw...

...a lolly stick.

That was all that was left of his ice lolly.

A small goat licked its lips.

It moved towards the lolly stick. It wanted to eat the stick too!

Mr Twaddle shooed it away.

Clive stood and stared at his lolly stick.

It was the sort of lolly stick that had a joke written on it, but it didn't cheer him up much.

He looked so fed up that even Miss Strictly felt sorry for him.

We'll get you another – Now where's that ice cream van?

'Never mind, Clive,' said David.

But Clive did mind. He minded
very much indeed.

Chapter 7

'Cheer up!' said David. 'You can read us the joke on your stick.'

Clive sighed and did as he was told.

The others knew the answer and they knew some more animal jokes.

How does a duck with no nose smell?
Terrible!
Why do cows have horns?
Because their bells don't work!
What do you get if you cross a cow and a sheep and a baby goat?
The Milky Bar kid!
CHOMP!
CHOMP!
What's green with hairy legs and stingers?
I don't know...
Neither do I - but one's just gone down your neck!

Clive thought of a new joke.
It wasn't actually about animals
but it was a good joke.

So they all had a good time
until Joanne said...

Chapter 8

Miss Strictly said, 'Time to fill in your question sheets.'

Clive was determined to do well.

So even when Gary was larking about,

Clive worked hard on his question sheet.

Even when Sally was chased by a sheep...

Clive worked hard on his question sheet.

And even when that goat tried to eat his shoelaces,

Clive worked hard on his question sheet.

He'd filled in all the gaps, answered all the questions and drawn rather a good duck.

So it was a pity his paper got…

…a little bit torn and messy.

And Miss Strictly was not pleased with him after all.

Then she said, 'Back on the bus everyone. We don't want to be late home.'

Chapter 9

The bus was hotter than ever. It had been standing in the sun all day long.

Clive shouted as he sat down on the hot seat.

While everyone else was singing or playing 'I Spy', Clive kept a lookout for the ice cream van.

But Miss Strictly said, 'Certainly not! We're all tired and hot and sticky and we want to get home.'

No one was tireder, or hotter, or stickier than Clive. And certainly no one was thirstier. But on they went until the bus started...

...hisssing and steaming, made a funny little hiccup and a splutter. WHOOSH KERPLUNK Hissssss...

And then it stopped.

'No,' explained the driver. 'It's such a hot day the *engine* has overheated. I'll have to get some water. I'll walk to a petrol station. You all stay on the bus. I should be about an hour… or so…'

The children groaned.

The helpful mothers groaned.

Even Miss Strictly groaned.

Then... 'I've got an idea,'
said Clive.

Chapter 10

Miss Strictly gave Clive permission to take the driver back to the ice cream van.

The sun beat onto the windows of the bus. Miss Strictly sighed. Everyone sighed.

She and everyone else waited in the stuffy bus

| They shuffled. | They waited. |

| They wilted. | They watched. |

And then...

Da da da dada da DA!!!

...over the hill came the ice cream van.

'Thank heavens,' said the helpful mothers.

'Thank Clive,' said Miss Strictly.

'Now I'll just get you that water,'
said the ice cream man.

'First things first,' said Miss Strictly.
'I want to buy everyone a nice cool ice
lolly. You all deserve one…'

HOORAY!!

Everyone cheered –
except for Clive.

Clive was too busy licking his

ice-cold nice-cold tangy fruity fresh fantastic ice lolly!!

Chapter 11

So at the end of the day everyone got home safely and no one was late – thanks to Clive. And Miss Strictly and all Clive's friends got together and made him a 'thank you' song.

47

About the author

This is my second story
about Clive, illustrated by
Dee Shulman.

My own first school trip
was to a stately home. We
spent ages on a bus, but
when we arrived we were
immediately sent home in
disgrace, because we'd
picked some flowers from the gardens.

The second trip was to a sewage works.
It rained all day. So I was very glad to write
about a school trip that has a happy ending.
I enjoyed writing about Clive again.